The Corgi Series

HARRI WEBB
The Stone Face

The Corgi Series   Writing from Wales

The Corgi Series  Writing from Wales

Harri Webb

The Stone Face and other poems

Series editor
Meic Stephens
Emeritus Professor of Welsh Writing in English
University of Glamorgan

Carreg Gwalch Cyf.

ISBN: 0-86381-717-3

Cover design: Sian Parri

Logo design: Dylan Williams

First published in 2004 by
Carreg Gwalch Cyf., 12 Iard yr Orsaf, Llanrwst,
Wales LL26 0EH
☏ 01492 642031   🖷 01492 641502
✆ books@carreg-gwalch.co.uk
website: www.carreg-gwalch.co.uk

Supported by an 'Arts for All' Lottery grant
from the Arts Council of Wales

Contents

Harri Webb (1920-94)

Harri Webb was the most popular Welsh poet in English of his generation. He was capable of writing in serious vein but deliberately chose to write verse that was easily understood, often witty and sometimes scathingly satirical. Among the forms he preferred were the rollicking ballad, the short squib and occasional verse celebrating a place, person or event, and he didn't mind if, on the page, some of his lines seemed a bit slapdash: they were meant to be read aloud. An erudite and sociable man, particularly late at night in convivial company, he could set the room laughing at his one-liners and the wicked fun he liked to poke at the pompous and powerful. Some of his poems, such as 'Ode to the Severn Bridge', are quoted in contexts where poetry is not often heard.

There is often a political slant to his work, whether Republican or Nationalist, for – like the Spanish and French writers he had studied – he saw little distinction between politics and poetry and took his role as People's Poet seriously: to inspire, inform and entertain his compatriots, or at least those who chose to take part in the struggle to win for Wales a degree of autonomy and a modicum of self-respect. He was active during the 1950s in the Welsh Republican Movement and thereafter as a leading member of Plaid Cymru. By profession he was a librarian, albeit with no formal qualifications, first in Dowlais and then at

Mountain Ash, where he is commemorated by a plaque in the foyer.

Born into a working-class home in the docklands of Swansea, to parents whose roots were in rural Gower, Harri won a scholarship to Magdalen College, Oxford, where he read Romance Languages, and served with the Navy during the second world war. He saw action during the battle for Crete, an experience that left a permanent mark on his nervous complexion, and was on the last boat out of Tobruk before it fell to the Germans. It was while wandering in Scotland, under the influence of the great poet Hugh MacDiarmid, that he decided to return to Wales and spend the rest of his life as a political activist.

One of the first things he did after demobilization was learn Welsh, a language that was always close to his heart, and join the Labour Party. But he grew disillusioned with that party's lukewarm support for Welsh self-government and threw in his lot with Plaid Cymru in 1960. A talented journalist and controversialist, he edited both *The Welsh Republican* and *Welsh Nation*. Selections of his political and literary journalism were published as *No Half-way House* and *A Militant Muse* respectively. He was much in demand as a public speaker who could use hyperbole and an impish sense of humour to excellent effect. In the 1970s he enjoyed a new career as a reader and writer for television, especially in the BBC programme *Poems and Pint* and as author of *How Green Was my Father*, starring the late Ryan Davies. His most famous poem is in Welsh: the haunting *'Colli Iaith'*, often sung by Heather Jones.

Harri once remarked that, as a poet, he had 'only one theme, one preoccupation' and that his work was 'unrepentantly nationalistic'. Most of his poems were written out of a deep and passionate commitment to the cause of Welsh independence. They have a historical perspective, as in 'The Stone Face' but are also aware of contemporary realities, as in 'A Crown for Branwen'. The scarred landscapes and radical traditions of the South Wales valleys, especially those of Merthyr, were a special source of inspiration for him and, in poems like 'Duffryn Woods', he managed to write delicately lyrical poems that are among his finest. His range of reference was wide and he drew on his knowledge of several languages and literatures. The many allusions in his poems are explained in the notes to his *Collected Poems* (1995).

At the end of his life, Harri chose to be moved to a nursing home in Swansea – he was always proud to call himself 'a Swansea Jack' – and a few weeks later was buried with his parents in the churchyard at Pennard in Gower. I was his friend for more than thirty years and one of the last things he said to me was: 'I've had my say. My stuff will be there when the Welsh need it.'

Tŷ Ddewi

Amazing blossom
In a southwest corner
Sprung from the rocks
At the touch of rain,
Coloured cathedral,
House of Dewi
In a sheltered valley,
Hidden and plain.

The tower too heavy
For your foundations
Sags with its heraldry,
The roof is askew,
On the soft green earth
Where you prayed and fasted
Your work is unfinished,
None fasts after you.

Our vows lie unbroken
About your altar
And your ashes on show
In a wooden box.
Restorers have silenced
Your well with rubble
But the spring runs clearly
Under the rocks.

Cold water, Dewi,
Is not for our palate,
We keep your festival
With foolish mirth,
Self-praise and self-pity,
Dragons and flagons,
But none who will suffer
For Wales in her dearth.

Pray for us, Dewi,
The undeserving,
The spring of our virtue
Leaks out in a fen.
Saint of pure water,
Instruct us in sacrifice
That the thirst of our land
May be slaked once again.

A Loyal Address

Queen of the rains and sorrows,
Of the steep and broken ways,
Lady of our tomorrows,
Redeem your yesterdays.

Queen of the gorse and heather,
Of the upraised unhewn stone,
Queen of the bitter weather,
We kneel before your throne.

Take us, there is no other
At whose feet we offer our pride,
Take us and break us, O Mother
For whom our fathers died.

While your eyes yet know not laughter,
While your lips speak but of pain,
All other tasks come after,
All other loves are vain.

Queen of the shadowed valleys,
Queen of the gates of the sea,
Rise up to the voice that rallies
The vanguard of the free.

When the night of the grey Iscariots
Lies dead in the red of our dawn,
Queen of the scythe-wheeled chariots,
Rise up, ride out, reborn!

Carmarthen Coast

Sea-hung cages of singing, hymn-barns
In villages of lace and brass and limewash
Look over the grey water. Held
In the lapse of a landscape's liquid outline,
The islands float in air.
In the steep hayfields, in the deep lanes
Where the primroses linger till autumn
And the white trefoils star the hedgerow grass,
Where all the flowers bloom at once and for ever,
You are near, but may not cross, the frontier of time.
Sweet heifers graze the saltings,
The tide laps at the roots of elder and thorn,
But the ferryman does not come to the ruined bellhouse.
You must stay
Or wander back to the parked car
In the lane that leads nowhere,
Gather the heavy blackberries
That grow only by this sea
In the queer light that shines only in this sky.
This is the edge of the world
Where you must mourn
For all you cannot escape from,
For all you have brought with you,
For Gwendraeth guilty with Gwenllian's blood,
For the silent sleepers under the green earth
Waiting, and waiting in vain,
For the named and the nameless,

For the smooth-tongued traitors and the dumb
                                    heroes,
For the white-robed riders by night
And the hands raised to curse at noon,
For all the starving ghosts and dead gods.
Fowls roost in the chancel, nettles grow on the altar
Where the saints fasted and the pilgrims prayed.
This sea will not cleanse you, and there is no
                                    forgiveness
In all the empty sky.
You have brought no prayers, no tears. You must
                                    return
To the towns without laughter and the valleys
                              without pride.

Local Boy Makes Good

When Christ was born on Dowlais Top
The ironworks were all on stop,
The money wasn't coming in,
But there was no room at the Half Moon Inn.

The shepherds came from Twyn y Waun
And three kings by the Merthyr and Brecon line,
The Star shone over the Beacons' ridge
And the angels sang by Rhymney Bridge.

When Christ turned water into stout
A lot of people were most put out
And wrote cross letters to the paper
Protesting at such a wicked caper.

When Christ fed the unemployed
The authorities were most annoyed;
He hasn't gone through the proper channels,
Said the public men on the boards and panels.

When Christ walked upon Swansea Bay
The people looked the other way
And murmured, This is not at all
The sort of thing that suits Porthcawl.

When Christ preached the sermon on Kilvey Hill
He'd have dropped dead if looks could kill
And as they listened to the Beatitudes
They sniffed with scorn and muttered, Platitudes!

When Christ was hanged in Cardiff Jail
Good riddance said the *Western Mail*,
But, daro, weren't all their faces red
When he came to judge the quick and the dead.

Valley Winter

Under the gas-lamps the wet brown fallen leaves
Glitter like glass of broken beer bottles;
The feast is finished, the hangover remains.
This is the time to walk the Welsh valleys
Under the rain that has been falling for ever
And the days that never dawn hiding the hills.
The mountains have vanished into another world,
The rivers boil black from hell under concrete bridges
And from the lost mountains ponies and sheep
                              come down,
Ghostly refugees in the streets that alone stand.
All the encompassing glory, the heroic crests
And soft voices of an older Wales are abolished
That we saw from every street-corner of our brief
                              summer,
And the black axemen have felled the singing forests.
One day we will climb again the cliffs of clear air,
Walk by the carolling water, redeem our strength
On the high places of the old gods and battles.
But, for now, only the streets are real
Where wet crowds shuffle shopping
And nobody sings or fights, not even the drunks,
Where we wait for buses that are never on time
And drag our feet through fallen, long-fallen leaves.

Big Night

We started drinking at seven
And went out for a breather at ten,
And all the stars in heaven
Said: Go back and drink again.

Orion was furiously winking
As he gave us the green light
So we went back in to our drinking
Through the breakneck Brecknock night.

We were singers, strongmen and sages,
We were witty and wise and brave,
And all the ghosts of the ages
Applauded from Crawshay's grave.

The tipsy Taff was bawling
A non-traditional tune
And the owls of Pontsarn were calling
Rude names at the frosty moon,

And homeward we were staggering
As the Pandy clock struck three
And the stars of the Plough went swaggering
From Vaynor to Pengarnddu.

The Cross Foxes

Come all valiant Welshmen, I'll tell you a tale
Of the boozing of beer and the swilling of ale,
'Twas in the Cross Foxes, the pride of fair Rhos,
We drank all they had and the pub had to close.

Hideho, Hidehi,
In Rhosllannerchrugog we drank the pub dry.

The National Eisteddfod was on Ponciau Flat
But Undeb y Tancwyr saw little of that,
They slept all the day and they drank all the night
The gin, rum and whisky, the dark and the light.

From Cardiff and Rhondda and Dowlais so fair
The principal pinters of Gwalia were there,
They gathered together and guzzled with glee
From the banks of the Teifi to the banks of the Dee.

Brave Yuri Gagarin he flew through the air
And saw all the jollification down there,
Said, It's all very well to be up in the sky
But I'd rather be helping to drink the pub dry.

The Gorsedd were marching with nightshirts so clean,
The sexiest sight that Rhos ever had seen,
Said Cynan, I think we're a wonderful lot –
But next to a woman I do like a pint pot.

The landlord he gave on the pump a last pull,
His cellar was empty, his till it was full,
The barmaid was fainting, the potman was weak –
Thank God the Eisteddfod's not here every week!

The Temperance Union they loved the sight
Of a pub with its doors shut on Saturday night,
They said, Carry on drinking without any pause,
You are doing great work for the Temperance Cause.

Romantic Peeps at Remote Peoples

I

We know the Etruscans only from their tombs,
They were a kindly people given to feasting,
To sport, conversation and the pleasures of love.
They excelled in some aspects of the minor arts
But were not very good at organization
And over-preoccupied, it seems, with death.
Their language lingered till historic times
But is now beyond reconstruction, quite extinct.
Their leading families, however, married
Into the Caesars, who could thus make claim
To be sort of Etruscan. They ruled the world
While the grass grew over their ancestral towns.

II

The paschal moon summons them from oblivion,
To its white face they lift the slaughtered lamb,
Old men in robes and turbans, Samaritans
Chanting a liturgy on Mount Gerizim
While keen photographers from *Paris-Match*
Capture the atmosphere of the scene.
But even in the Bible these were heretics
And have been stagnating for two thousand years
In their dead end. Their ceremonial tabernacles
Are English Army surplus bell-tents,
Their scriptures are a mediaeval fake,
They are degenerate from inbreeding,
Are maintained by charity and will soon die out.

III

Acknowledging the undoubted place of God,
It is more prudent to conciliate
His Adversary, say the Yezidi Kurds,
An interesting tribe of Manichees
Who claim, with every show of commonsense,
The Devil rules the world, whoever made it.
But nobody could call them diabolic,
Pathetic would be nearer the truth.
They are poor, ignorant and quite confused,
Not at all sure which obscure sheikh it is
Whose simple shrine serves as their meeting place
To venerate the serpent and the peacock.

IV

Of these a Roman writer has recorded
They fought well among their native forests
But fighting retail were beaten wholesale.
A thousand years later, one of their own sort
Told them, if they would be inseparable
Then would they be insuperable. But
They seem to have been incurably perverse,
Not uniquely so, but certainly fatally.
They have left few traces and these unremarkable,
Which is strange, considering they were said to be,
In their day, a vivid people.

The Nightingales

Once there were none and the dark air was dumb
Over the tree-stumps, the bare deforested hills.
They were a legend that the old bards had sung,
Gone now, like so much, so much.
But once I heard them drilling away the dark,
Llandâf was loud with them all of a summer's night
And the great Garth rose like a rock from their storm.
This most of all I desire: to hear the nightingales
Not by Taff only but by all our streams,
Black Rhymni, sullen Ogwr, dirty Ebbw,
Dishonoured Tawe and all our sewered drabs.
And others whose names are an unvisited music
(Wales, Wales, who can know all your rivers?),
The nightingales singing beyond the Teifi,
By Aeron, Ystwyth, Rheidol, and those secret waters
The Beacons hold: Rhiangoll, Tarrell, Crawnon,
By Heptse and Mellte outstanding Scwd Einion Gam
(But let them not sing by Elan, Claerwen, Fyrnwy
Or Tryweryn of the Shame.)
You who have outsung all our dead poets,
Sing for them again in Cwm Prysor and Dyffryn
                                                   Ceiriog,
And humble Gwydderig and Creidiol, do not
                                       forget them.
And that good man, no poet, who gave us a song
Even sweeter than yours, sing for him at
                                       Llanrhaeadr,

And in Glyndyfrdwy, what need to tell you to sing?
Sing in the faded lands, Maelienydd and Elfael,
And in the plundered cantrefs that have no name.
Come back and sing to us, we have waited too long,
For too long have not been worth singing for.
The magic birds that sang for heroes in Harlech
And hushed to wonder the wild Ardudwy sea
And they of Safaddan that sing only for princes,
We cannot call them again, but come you
And fill our hearts like the hearts of other men.
Shall we hear you again soon, soon?

A Voice in the Wind

The wind blows in old memories like dead leaves,
Inconsequential, tumbling, then one sticks
Tapping, tapping, impossible to dislodge,
Places, names, none of them somehow quite
The expected visitor. They've been there all the time
Whirling about in the dark, now they won't go,
Tapping, tapping, names, memories.
The wind in my roof tonight blows in from the
                                            Waun Pound,
High common above three valleys crammed
With small houses and huge wrongs, the air
Brisk, the northern crop of the coal-measures,
Abrupt frontier between slag-heaps and rough
                                            pasture.
That's where I saw you, heard you, shook your hand.
Our paths touched an instant, that was all.
You stood on the back of a lorry, spoke to a crowd
Of perhaps a thousand, a politician in a smart suit,
Master of oratory, at home, confident, in command,
The world was listening. Unconsciously I noted
Your back was turned to the hills, you gestured
Always to the valleys below. You spoke of a dream,
Summoning your people – yes, they were your people,
Yours, and you were their leader, you held them
In the hollow of your hand – to build anew
Where the old tyrants had cheated and despoiled.
The crowd was silent. It could have been a scene

Any time in our history, the chieftain aloft
And the host mustered to follow.

Already though,
It was something of a sentimental pilgrimage,
The spot chosen because here in the starving years
The gaunt contingents had converged from Rhymni,
Tredegar, Ebbw Vale, the Valleys of the Shadow,
To seek a dawn, and even on that day
Of sunshine and solidarity, there was somehow
The breath of premonition that all too soon
There would be no more such meetings, nor no man
Like this one to inspire them, and the people
Would have found other places to go, the Waun
                                   Pound
As unregarded as in the time before the first forges
Flamed in Gwent. Here and there in the crowd
The older men whispered this behind their hands
And drew their belted raincoats closer around them.
But I will not begrudge you or myself the bright
                                   memory
Of Aneurin Bevan standing against the sky,
A Silurian prince, even though you lost your way.

Influence

I dreamt last night that Keir Hardie's ghost
Applied for a Merthyr Borough post;
He didn't get it, what a pity,
But look who's chairman of the committee.

Above Tregaron

This is a way to come in winter. This is a way
Of steep gradients, bad corners for cars,
It is metalled now, but this is a way
Trodden out by cattle, paced yet by the ghosts
Of drovers. The valleys ring with echoes,
When the car-horn sounds, of wise horsemen
Calling across the streams, the slow black herds
Steaming and jostling, the corgi's yelp.
The sweet breath of cows still hangs in the air
Between rock, bracken and milk-foamed water.
Away from the road stand the farmhouses,
The loneliest it is said, even in this land
Of lonely places, and on the high ground
Between Irfon and Camddwr you are as far away
As you will ever be from the world's madness.
The drivers you pass wave and nod a greeting,
Recreating you as a person from a statistic.
Look on it for the last time; in a few years
The pinetrees will have hidden it in their darkness.

Even now perhaps it is not quite right
To take this road when there are easier routes.
Flying from madness, maybe we bring it with us,
Patronising romantics, envying the last survivors
Of an old way of life, projecting our dreams
On this conveniently empty scenery, deserted
By its sons for the hard bright streets we come from.
We pass them perhaps on the road, our journey
An interlude, theirs a beginning, an end.
Pause on the watershed, look round, pass on,
Leave it behind. Anyway, it's all dead, you'll tell me,
Like everything else traditional in Wales
And not before time too. That is why I say
This is a way to come in winter.

By a Mountain Pool

Now by this sulky mountain pool I pause.
Its waters are as dark and deep a blue
As if it were the sea, but it is shallow,
A gathering of rains, a sheep pond only,
Yet, even in the mist, ultramarine
As deep and dark as if it were the sea.
Is this my country's image? Have I leapt
Into a fancied ocean, sink or swim,
Only to stumble in a shallow pool
And suffocate in mud? Yet even now
The water is so blue it seems a jewel
Lost by a god here on the high wet moors.
Be you my mirror, lakelet of the mountains,
Now as I raise my wearied hands to lift
The heavy dragon helmet form my shoulders
For the last time.
                    It was not always so.
A plain steel helmet hastily adorned
With Corwen smith-work was my only crown
When those lads rode with me from Glyndyfrdwy
Up to the Clwydian hills and made me king.
And when the land was ours they gave me a crown
Of fine French jewelry, and this great dragon helm
To guard that crown, the golden crown of Wales.
And when I drove the English from the land
And seemed to command the lightning and the
                                        thunder,

And when my star burned over burning castles,
Then was the hour of the dragon, my blazing crest.
And in the long retreat from the fickle south,
The bargaining west, the supine central valleys,
The steadfast men who carried in their swords
The soul of Wales kept their eyes on the dragon
And held their heads up proudly as they rode
With Owain into the mist, where now I wander,
An old man, alone by a mountain pool,
The mirror of an ageing face, white hair
That shone red-gold in the breeze of the Clwydian
                                                                    hills
When I was crowned with steel.
                                                For all too long
I have looked out on the world through helmet bars,
My voice has echoed iron in command
Out from the faceless helm, even to myself
An iron voice, echoing inside my skull.
But now the iron echoes die away;
Unhelmeted, I see my face in the pool
With no bars in between, no dragon crest
Ramping implacably above my head,
An old man's face, seen in a mountain pool,
And every furrow of age and scar of battle
The dark water deepens, and my eyes
Are shadow, bottomless shadow that goes down
Deeper than the water that reflects them.
The great helm here in the crook of my arm
At last now bears too heavy for my age,

A thing of rusted steel and faded crest
That should hang honourably in an old man's hall
And hang at last in church over his tomb.
But I can have no certain resting place
And Owain's grave must always be unknown.
The hall is not yet built, the church not hallowed
That dares to house the royalty of Wales.
This pool's the place, no shepherd wandering here,
No anxious traveller, no hastening drover
Will ever spare a glance or a stray thought
For this blue scrap of water. Only the flocks
And waterfowl will trouble it at the edge
And never know what greatness is drowned here.
It is best so. All strife, all hope is drowned.
I give it to the keeping of the mountains,
I give it to the keeping of the waters.
I quench the heraldry of sovereign Wales
Here in this pool. So. It is gone. It is done.
The dragon's fire is out. Now I ride home
Bareheaded, the wet mist beading my hair.
And as the iron echoes die away
The wind stirs in the mist and in the wind –
Voices.

   Owain!

    Voices, voices I hear
From nowhere.

     From afar.

       This cannot be.
I wore the great helmet too long, the echoing iron,

And am haunted now by echoes of old voices
Out of the past.
                    Out of the future, Owain.
We speak from the unbuilt cities, from a time unborn,
From beyond experience, beyond imagination.

You speak to mock me, an old broken man.
But no, these are not fiends' voices. Blazon
                              yourselves,
Your names, your nation and your quality.

It is enough that you should know our nation.
Our names are a ragman roll and our quality
No better, but our nation is your nation.

It lives beyond this darkness? Beyond the ruin
Of town and farm? Beyond the death I made?

Because you made this death the nation lives.

After this dark night, there came a dawn?

After this dark night there came a darker,
And darkness on darkness and then a long dawn,
A struggling sickly dawn as long as the darkness.

But where you speak from, does the sun now shine?

We have caught at last a glimpse of the red sun

And its redness is the colour of the dragon
Drowned by a fugitive prince in a moorland pool.

How are you mustered? What is your armament?
What bards sing you to battle? What allies?

Our friends are few and hard-pressed as ourselves.
Our strength is our own, none other and none the worse.

I know you are indeed my nation. Speak on.

Beyond the darkness: beyond the mists of morning,
By the farthest shore and in the inmost valleys,
We muster to your summons and to the call
Of all the other captains of our people
From those first swords that lit the fires of dawn
When we held out against the brazen eagles
From the hot south and from the hungry north
The harsh black ravens to that weary day
That falls to us, the day of the drab vultures,
The carrion breed of Mersey and of Thames,
The living dead, the songless bringers of silence.
We send our message to you across time
That is halted for ever in the heart of our wild hills,
To you alone by a mountain pool in the mist
From the cities of neon and nylon, the glass battlements
From a land besieged, seduced by alien witchcraft,
Against a taller terror than ever strode
In armour through the woods or beached the longships,

A shy assault of black legality
That wears no blazoned baldric nor horned hat
But brings a surer death than ever their swords.

He too I had to face. At Croesau Common
My proud neighbour, Grey of Ruthun, invoked him
And sent me home insulted from his court.
But I burnt Ruthun and I beggared Grey.
And more than Croesau Common were in the
                                                    balance,
But all the lands of Wales, was it ours or theirs?
But I was a young man then. Now I am old and
                                                    finished.
Leave me in peace. Why do you call on me?
I failed.

> *It is not we who call on you*
But you on us, that we must keep faith with Owain
Or die shamed.

I drowned it, I tell you, here in the mist.
In a mountain pool I drowned my faith and my
                                                    kingdom.
They are gone like water. Let the water keep them.
How can they rise again?

> *They rise again from the water,*
From all the waters of Wales, from all the rivers,
Her torrent brooks, her lakes, her mountain pools.

Where the mist rises at evening or dawn
The warriors ride again along the valleys:
Wherever water speaks by a bridge in the twilight
Or whispers on gravel at noon, it is a voice
That hisses shame on those who keep no faith,
It is a voice that never can be silenced.
It is your voice, Owain.

I give you my voice again:
Fight on. You have kept faith with me, I will
Keep faith with you. Wherever you strike in
                              vengeance
My strength is in your arm. You have come to me
In a chill twilight, from deep in the pool of the sleep
Of the dragon.

That does not sleep.

You have come to call me
To the battle I had thought ended when the last
Blow was struck on the banks of Monmouth river.

Owain, the rivers of Wales are numberless
And every river a battle, and every battle a song.
Our bards shall string their harps with battles and rivers
And you shall ride with us, fording them one by one
As we take them, one by one, back into our keeping.

The Boomerang in the Parlour

Will Webb, a farmer's son from the cliffs of Gower,
Went as a young man to Australia, exchanging
The cramped peninsula for the outback, the frugal
Patchwork of fields for the prodigal spaces he rode
Along the rabbit-fence or under the soaring jarra.
When he came back he brought with him a
                        boomerang
For the front-room mantelpiece, a spearhead
                    chipped by an abo
From the green glass of a beer-bottle, an emu-skin
                          rug
And the poems of Banjo Paterson. To me, his son,
He looked for the completion of a journey
Stopped at Gallipoli, that in my turn I'd see
The river of black swans. The map of Australia
Was tattooed on his right arm.
                       And so I have
Another hypothetical Australian self,
The might-have-been man of a clean new empty
                    country
Where nearly all the songs have yet to be sung.
It is this shadow that perhaps has led me
Past islands of enchantment, capes that could have
                    been
Called deception, disappointment and farewell,
To the strange and silent shore where now I stand,
Terra Incognita: a land whose memory

Has not begun, whose past has been forgotten
But for a clutter of nightmares and legends and lies.
This land, too, has a desert at its heart.

The Hill

Llanddewi Brefi. Winter. Early dusk.
An empty church looming too large
For the village on its dark hill
That rose to Dewi's prayer.
Heavy Victorian railings, a steep
Gravel path between tilted graves.
The place is silent after evensong.
Switch on the light. Here are the arches
Of the *clas* rich in leadmines and bees,
The Mothers' Union banner, the memorials
Of a squandered squirearchy patching
The wall inscribed also by the Second
Asturian Cohort, in the porch
The old stone monuments rescued
From the weather like hill sheep
Penned for a show, debased Roman
Capitals deeply and coarsely cut,
Idnert who was killed, Dumelus,
An Irish name, and in the nave
Dewi, carved in white stone, the gift
Of a good churchwoman, the latest
Treasure bestowed on a dark hill
Older than creed or language,
Holier than any god.

Thanks in Winter

The day that Eliot died I stood
By Dafydd's grave in Ystrad Fflur,
It was the depth of winter,
A day for an old man to die.
The dark memorial stone,
Chiselled in marble of Latin
And the soft intricate gold
Of the old language
Echoed the weather's colour,
A slate vault over Ffair Rhos,
Pontrhydfendigaid, Pumlumon,
The sheep-runs, the rough pasture
And the lonely whitewashed houses
Scattered like frost, the dwellings
Of country poets, last inheritors
To the prince of song who lies
Among princes among ruins.
A pilgrim under the yew at Ystrad Fflur
I kept my vow, prayed for my country,
Cursed England, came away

And home to the gas fire and television
News. Caught between two languages,
Both dying, I thanked the long-dead
Minstrel of May and the newly silent
Voice of the bad weather, the precise
Accent of our own time, taught
To the disinherited, offering
Iron for gold.

Cilmeri

In the nameless years shapeless as sand-dunes
Oblivion drifted over Aberffraw, the four-sided grave
On the banks of the Alaw gave up the dust of Branwen
But the stone coffins rang empty of the bones
Of fallen princes, dead principalities.
The hall brought from Conwy to the hold
Of the stone battleship moored below Segontium
Is unaccounted for. An ignorant past
Careless of its idiot plunder, spendthrift
Even of David's Sapphire and the Croes Naid,
Has squandered our treasure, bestowed on harlotry
The wages of our blood, sold in the market-place
The decent things of our people for beer and beads.

So we have come to this. There is nothing left
Tangible, no way of speech or thought or song
That is valid any more. There is only death, ours,
The nation's, and all the deaths for her sake.
So we have come to this stone. In the time
Of yellow grass, no flowers, iron earth. So
We have come.

Here is only stone, water and death,
In a dead season. There is no guarantee
That anything will come of this; no sacrament
Is valid any more. The slack dunes
Spread further inland, the wells turn brackish

Or dry up. Here is the heart of the hills
Where the strategic roads converged to crucify:
A stone, water, words.
In the cold air the words fall like stones
In water: a splash, a ripple of rings,
A brief erosion. But the echo rouses
The sleeping augural birds, and suddenly
The sky is full of wings.

Progress

Hooray for English culture,
To Wales it's such a blessing:
Tuneless songs and tasteless jokes
And blowzy bags undressing.

Vive Le Sport!

Sing a song of rugby,
Buttocks, booze and blood,
Thirty dirty ruffians
Brawling in the mud.

When the match is over
They're at the bar in throngs,
If you think the game is filthy,
Then you should hear the songs.

The Old Parish Churchyard

I share this churchyard Sunday silence with
A nibbling sheep, another stray presence
Whose mind inherits a pattern laid down
Before Tydfil's bones. Now we both browse
About her abandoned altar. The crisp cropping
Is louder than the traffic that buzzes
Around the roundabout just beyond the railings
Massive with rust. A few yards of grass
And straggling nameless bushes insulate
The churchyard, the Sunday, the afternoon
From a world in which there are no more
Churchyards, Sundays or afternoons.

Here they all lie, the people Of This Village,
Of This Parish, under flaking local stone
Lettered in simple elegance in the
Ceremonial English of the Welsh-speaking dead:
The farmers, the lieutenants of industry
(The captains, of course, are interred elsewhere),
Some who did good, remembered by the student,
But mostly forgotten, and even these names
Only the literate generations floodlit
Between the green committals and the crematoria
Of all the dead of Wales, a land where only
The dead are secure in their inheritance.
Caved-in table-tombs, expressive once
Of aspirations in a social order, up-end

Their rotten limestone in untidy chaos.
Frost and neglect have eroded the epitaphs
Composed with such care, and now nobody bothers
Even to desecrate. The kindly, tired grass
Is doing its best to hide total abandonment.

Outside the churchyard wall the new flats
Rear their functional hutches, the smooth roads
Sweep over the old slums. Along the river bank
The rubble of the past is pounded to foundations
For a better world. Up on the White Tip,
Ridges of late snow gleam in weak sunshine
Like tattered banners in an old battle.
A sly wind snipes from the river Taff;
There are withdrawals, advances, but, in this land,
No victory, no defeat. At my approach
The sheep lifts her head, her twin lambs
Start up from the tombstones and scamper in their
                                                    spring.

Dyffryn Woods

for Robert Morgan, who asks, from exile,
How are the Dyffryn trees now?

In perfect equipoise a moment
Between the green leaf and the brown,
The Dyffryn trees still stand in beauty
About the mean and straggling town,

Last of the spreading woods of Cynon
Our nameless poet loved and sung,
Calling a curse on their despoilers,
The men of iron heart and tongue,

In stillness at the end of autumn
They wait to see the doom fulfilled,
The final winter of the townships
When the last pithead wheels are stilled.

Our earth, though plundered to exhaustion,
Still has the strength to answer back,
In houses built above the workings
The roof-trees sag, the hearth-stones crack.

Soon the last coaltruck down the valley
Will leave the sidings overgrown,
While through the streets of crumbling houses
The old men crawl with lungs of stone.

And now as in the long green ages
The Dyffryn trees stand full and tall,
As lovely as in exile's memory,
Breathless, a breath before the fall.

Epil y Filiast

Already something of a stranger now,
A spry old man is walking his milgi out
Of a Sunday morning when the nineteenth century
Is in chapel and the twentieth in bed.
But his morning is centuries younger than these
As he steps it out and the lean dog lopes beside him
To fields where it will flash and pounce and double
As once in Glyn Cuch Woods.
And the old man stands in his grubby mackintosh
With a jaunty set to his shoulders,
A clean white scarf around his withered throat
And his cap on one side – *ticyn slic*.
His whistle carries further than the rotting pitheads,
The grass-grown tips, the flashy, flimsy estates.
He is a gambler, a drinker, a doggy-boy,
Better at drawing the dole than earning a wage.
The supermarket rises where Calfaria stood,
To him it is all one, he is older than any of it.
Mark him well, he is the last of his kind,
The last heir of Cadwaladr, Caswallon
And all our dead princes.

Patagonia

Teaspoon and tablespoon, towels, plates,
Blankets, a cup and saucer rather large,
Knife and fork, a boiling pot, a quart tin
And one that would hold three gallons;
With these, a tailor, printer, shoemaker,
A saddler, shopkeepers and coalminers
From Mountain Ash, quarrymen, ministers
Conquered a wilderness. They slept
The first night in caves. When Mrs Davies
Called to the cows (in Welsh, of course)
Come here my girl, come along my fine girl,
The herd stampeded. The gauchos taught them,
Before milking, lasso and tether.
They planted vegetables but nothing grew
Because there was no rain. It was Aaron Jenkins
From Troedyrhiw who first cut a channel
That brought floodwater to his parched wheat.
The Indians came, trading skins and feathers
For cloth and bread, they could hardly believe
That these were Christians. Over the huts
A flag flew that was older than Christ.
The first thing a later traveller saw was:
Clean, lately washed pink garments fluttering
From a clothesline. I had not seen such a sight
Through the whole of South America . . . The
                                       atmosphere
Is wholesome, clean and indisputably Welsh.

They pressed on to the foothills of the Andes
Naming the nameless places: Throne of Clouds,
The Valley Beautiful. They are there today,
Prosperous farmers writing in the style of Ceiriog.

Who now will conquer the wilderness of Wales?

Ode to the Severn Bridge

Two lands at last connected
Across the waters wide,
And all the tolls collected
On the English side.

The Stone Face

discovered at Deganwy, Spring 1966

It may of course be John his father-in-law,
Their worst, our best, not easily discernible
After so many buried centuries. The experts
Cannot be sure, that is why they are experts.
But this stone face under a broken crown
Is not an impersonal mask of sovereignty;
This is the portrait of a living man,
And when his grandson burnt Deganwy down
So that no foreign army should hold its strength,
I think they buried the head of Llywelyn Fawr
As primitive magic and for reasons of state.

No fortress was ever destroyed so utterly
As was Deganwy by Llywelyn the Last,
The thoroughness of despair, foreknown defeat,
Was in the burning and breaking of its walls.
But at some door or window a hand paused,
A raised crowbar halted by the stare
Of a stone face. The Prince is summoned
And the order given: Bury it in the earth,
There will be other battles, we'll be back –
Spoken in the special Welsh tone of voice
Half banter, half blind fervour, the last look
Exchanged between the hunted living eyes
And dead majesty for whom there are no problems.

The burning of Deganwy, the throne and fortress
Of Llywelyn Fawr shattered, his principality
Gone in the black smoke drifting over Menai
And his last heir forced into endless retreat
To the banks of Irfon and the final lance-thrust.
There was no return, no reverent unearthing.

A stone face sleeps beneath the earth
With open eyes. All history is its dream.
The Great Orme shepherds the changing weather,
On Menai's shores the tides and generations
Ebb, grumble and flow; harps and hymns
Sound and fall silent; briefly the dream flares out of
                                    the eyes
Then darkness comes again.

Seven hundred and fifty years of darkness.
Now in a cold and stormy Spring we stand
At the unearthing of the sovereign head,
The human face under the chipped crown.
Belatedly, but not too late, the rendez-vous is made.
The dream and the inheritors of the dream,
The founder and father, and those who must rebuild
The broken fortress, re-establish the throne
Of eagles, here exchange the gaze of eagles
In the time of the cleansing of the eyes.

Colli Iaith

Colli iaith a cholli urddas
Colli awen, colli barddas
Colli coron aur cymdeithas
Ac yn eu lle cael bratiaith fas.

Colli'r hen alawon persain
Colli tannau'r delyn gywrain
Colli'r corau'n diaspedain
Ac yn eu lle cael clebar brain.

Colli crefydd, colli enaid
Colli ffydd yr hen wroniaid
Colli popeth glân a thelaid
Ac yn eu lle cael baw a llaid.

Colli tir a cholli tyddyn
Colli Elan a Thryweryn
Colli Claerwen a Llanwddyn
A'n gwlad i gyd dan ddŵr llyn.

Cael yn ôl o borth marwolaeth
Cân a ffydd a bri yr heniaith
Cael yn ôl yr hen dreftadaeth
A Chymru'n dechrau ar ei hymdaith.

Israel

Listen, Wales. Here was a people
Whom even you could afford to despise,
Growing nothing, making nothing,
Belonging nowhere, a people
Whose sweat-glands had atrophied,
Who lived by their wits,
Who lived by playing the violin
(A lot better, incidentally,
Than you ever played the harp).
And because they were such a people
They went like lambs to the slaughter.

But some survived (yes, listen closer now),
And these are a different people,
They have switched off Mendelssohn
And tuned in to Maccabeus.
The mountains are red with their blood,
The deserts are green with their seed.
Listen, Wales.

Manuscript Found in a Bottle

Memory, that old anarchist, keeps no rules,
Is no respecter of conventional wisdom. Memory
Is a gate-crasher, a dirty joker, a death's head.
For instance, all my recollections of the Holy Land
Should be, well, not exactly holy, but at least
Respectable, part of a pattern, bearing some relation
To the Good Book or Current Affairs. Deep down
Perhaps some potent apocalypse is still brewing
But somehow I hope not. It is better this way,
With all my memories rather disreputable –
Getting pissed in the Palestine Police Barracks
The Stern Gang later blew up – or wildly farcical
Like that Sunday on Haifa quay when a Bishop
Preached to the Second Cruiser Squadron, drawn up
All blanco and bullshit with our scruffier mob,
The Fifth Destroyer Flotilla, all boiled raw
In the stinking heat, his asinine Anglican accent
Nagging God like a public school prefect. His sermon
Was about Origen. How he went on as we sweated
And craved for our grog. You'd have thought, really,
That Celsus was a paid-up Obergruppenfuhrer.
He didn't tell all the truth about him, though,
That he'd cut off his balls to make sure of being holy.
Perhaps it was just as well, given the congregation,
I don't somehow think they'd have seen the point.
Yes, my memories are true ones. I avoided
All shrines, tombs, temples, pilgrimages,

Was resolutely profane, chose to take my liberty
In Tel Aviv, on the beach and in the nightclubs
Rather than the other places. Anyway, we all
                              wanted out.
The dour drab Jews meant just as much to us
And just as little, as the picturesque Arabs.
Let the fuckers fight it out themselves, we said.
Even then our money was on Moshey. Jack was wiser
Than those set in authority over him.
(Years later
I saw, in a newsreel, Haifa docks again,
An old man with a long beard, straight off the boat
Knelt down and kissed the railway lines. Talk
                              about laugh.)
Raffish memories, welcome like old mates,
Once you were not mere shades, but life itself.
Asserting against all history's prestige
That everything begins now, from where you are.
I think, too, as we gossip together a little
Before you scamper back to wherever it is
You plan your next surprise, how irrelevant
A place can be when you're there, if it isn't yours,
It's only when you get back you see what matters
And that the real truth begins and ends at home.

Not to be Used for Babies

Old Glyn, our milkman, came from down the country
Between Waun-arlwydd and Mynydd Bach y Glo,
A neighbour of innumerable uncles and cousins
In an untidy region of marsh and pasture and mines.
He spoke Welsh, of course, but was frequently too
                                                    drunk
To talk in any language. His milk, though, was good
And his measure generous, as he splashed it into
                                                the jug
From a bright battered can with a big extra splash
For a good boy. The spokes of his light trap
And the big brass churn amidships shone in the sun
And his brisk mare Shân was a champion trotter;
And when I took the reins of a Saturday morning
(With Glyn's big paw still on them, just in case)
I drove the chariot of the sun, I was Caesar, Ben Hur,
I was a big boy, helping the milkman.
My parents said among themselves it was drink,
When Glyn stopped coming. I think it was the bottles
And the new ways, the zombie electric trolley,
The precisely measured pints. Nobody is cheated now,
There is nothing extra, splashed out in good will
For a good boy. I buy my milk in a tin.
It is a dry powder. They have ground Glyn's bones.

Jack Frost and Sally Sunshine

a song for Lowri Angharad

Jack Frost and Sally Sunshine
Are not the best of friends,
Jack Frost gets up in the morning
And nips your finger ends.

But then comes Sally Sunshine,
Shaking her golden curls,
Dancing on walls and hedges,
Smiling on boys and girls.

Jack Frost he is an artist,
He's busy through the night
And with a brush of magic
He paints the windows white.

But Sally has no patience
With the patterns Jack has made,
She breathes upon the windows
And all the pictures fade.

Jack Frost is fond of winter sports
And he'll make you a fine slide,
But Sally warms the summer sea
For splashing in the tide.

Jack Frost lives up on Dowlais Top
And Sally down in Barry,
Its just as well they're far apart –
Those two will never marry.

But sometimes in the springtime
And sometimes in autumn weather,
Jack Frost and Sally Sunshine
Come out and play together.

When white frost sparkles on the grass
And sunshine gilds the wall,
Then's the best time for playing,
Then's the best time of all.

Synopsis of the Great Welsh Novel

Dai K lives at the end of a valley. One is not quite sure
Whether it has been drowned or not. His Mam
Loves him too much and his Dada drinks.
As for his girlfriend Blodwen, she's pregnant. So
Are all the other girls in the village – there's been a
Revival.
After a performance of Elijah, the mad preacher
Davies the Doom has burnt the chapel down.
One Saturday night after the dance at the Con Club,
With the Free Wales Army up to no good in the
back-lanes,
A stranger comes to the village; he is, of course,
God, the well-known television personality. He
succeeds
In confusing the issue, whatever it is, and departs
On the last train before the line is closed.
The colliery blows up, there is a financial scandal
Involving all the most respected citizens; the Choir
Wins at the National. It is all seen, naturally,
Through the eyes of a sensitive boy who never
grows up.
The men emigrate to America, Cardiff and the
moon. The girls
Find rich and foolish English husbands. Only daft
Ianto
Is left to recite the Complete Works of Sir Lewis
Morris

To puzzled sheep, before throwing himself over
The edge of the abandoned quarry. One is not quite
                                                 sure
Whether it is fiction or not.

Heat Wave

The hot weather, to which we are unaccustomed,
Puts me in mind of you, Gruffydd Robert, exile
In sweltering Italy for your faith, confessor to
The Most Magnificent Lord, Carlo Borromeo,
Prince of the Church, Archbishop of Milan, architect
Of the Counter-Reformation, entombed, sculptured
In the high baroque under those clustered spires,
The crown of Lombardy, teacher of children, friend
Of the poor, and when the plague struck up out of
The foul heat, a hero of Christ. He too at Trent
Shaped and shouldered the monumental marble
Blocks of dogma, slammed-to the clanging portcullis
Of the definitive creeds. You were with him in it all,
You, minor poet in a proscribed language, fugitive
From second-generation London-Welsh arrivistes
And their ballock-built religion. You left us,
                        ultimately,
To Calvin and his hatchet-men, but all these
                        squabbles
Are dead now, they tell us. Only the exile remains,
                        only
The loneliness that speaks across the centuries,
                        across
The paper walls of dialectic to the heart's depths
That are one for ever, our heart, our being
One with all who have ever loved and will love
Wales.

It is there in the preface to your Grammar
Mixed up with your plans for the language, a sheer
Physical lust for this land and its known weather.
You sweated your exile out, speaking bad Italian
Under those jewelled heavens the painters made an
image
Of Heaven itself. You would have given it all
For one glimpse of the ragged grey storm sky,
A sopping homespun blanket over bleak moorland.
Your faith sustained you, chaplain to a saint
At the centre of civilization, but always longing
For the land that is not quite of Europe, not quite
Of anywhere, not quite even itself.
Unseasonable
Even in summer, the great heat reminds me
Of places where it is always like this, hot rock,
Acrid dust, the sun a cynical tyrant, the lands
Of holy antiquity, impressive remains, the vine and
olive,
Continuous tradition, grace, arrogance, polyphony.
Corralled in England's backyard, then as now, you
saw us
One with the great sweep of Renaissance culture, one
In the Mass, heirs of all that reason and faith
Had given to man. Well, in the end I suppose,
We found our own way to it. Did you ever,
I wonder, catch an echo of the waterfall music,
The cataract that thundered out of Llanrhaeadr,

Among the formal fountains, the Word of God in
                                          Welsh
That William Morgan, Puritan Protestant, unleashed,
As you paced where a thirsty country orchestrated
Its thin rainfall in precise parabola? Will I,
An Anglican atheist writing in the wrong language,
                                          exile,
In the way of my century, here at home, earn
                                          something
Of the understanding I feel for you, when future
                                          men,
If there are any, read of my dreams? You are my
                                          guarantee,
Now as the Tridentine absolutes dissolve in acid fog,
That the heart's truth is a sure compass pointing
To the central star that shines above all shipwreck.

Cwm Tâf Bridge

for Penri Williams

It's fifteen years since we had a summer so dry
That the bridge at Cwmtâf rose to human eye
Above the reservoir water, and they say, before
That, it hadn't been seen for fifteen years more.
We made our way to it across the dried mud
And in a quiet evening of July we stood
On the loosened stonework, watched the fish rise
Breaking the level water, snapping at gnats and flies.
From the crumbled parapet a couple of night lines
                                        were out,
Somebody hoping to catch an illegal trout.
And we traced the line of a road coming down to
                                        the river
And talked of things that are gone now for ever
Under the reservoir, how the bridge in the old days
Was the meeting-place of all the country ways
For flirting and fighting or just spitting in the stream,
And how old people's memories are no more than
                                        a dream.
And as we savoured the cool evening calm
You told me the names and families of every farm
Whose ghostly rubble glimmered above the river banks
Where the pinetrees marshalled their mathematical
                                        ranks.

In the last light a buzzard hovered on outstretched wings
Over the dead homes where nobody sows or sings.
Far distant, it seemed, occasional traffic went by,
The water at our feet mirrored the darkening sky,
Down to the dam's hard outline stretching away,
A lake of hushed twilight, pearl and silver-grey –
The bounty of nature harnessed for the works of man.
We could see down the valley to the tip above Aberfan.
We stayed there a long time, not talking much aloud.
The evening, the lake, the hills, were suddenly a shroud.

The Island

Why does an island
Suddenly surface
After twenty-five years
Sunk in oblivion?
A place I went to
And came away from
Empty, a replica
Of what it once had been,
Tastefully restored
For loud-voiced ladies
With good tweeds and plain faces,
A place of pilgrimage
For antiquarians
And modish mystics,
Too small, too beautiful
To be really relevant,
The silver beaches,
The sapphire sea,
The emerald grass,
Too good to be true,
And the redcoat phone-box,
Sassenach sentry,
Conscripted the youngsters
To talk to the mainland
Where they soon would go,
Leaving their island
To gushing tourists.

Even its history
Seemed overstated,
Typically Celtic;
From the little hill
Called Farewell-to-Eire
The coast of Ireland
Is perfectly visible,
A few hours sailing
Even in a coracle.
Yet this was the scene
Of Goodbye For Ever,
Eternal exile
In the grand manner.
And over to Staffa
The sly sea fiddled
Perfect Mendelssohn.
I went as I came
Having learnt nothing
But silly legends,
For all it has meant to me
It could have been anywhere
Tediously famous,
Piccadilly Circus
Or the Grand Canyon.
Yet now, here in Wales,
This scrap of Scotland
Is alive, fermenting,
Flung up in my mind
By hidden fires.

The tides boil around her,
Her bright escarpments
Focus the sun,
With all the crash
Of delayed impact
Iona explodes.

The Red, White and Green

On the first day of March we remember
St David the pride of our land,
Who taught us the stern path of duty
And for freedom and truth made a stand.

So here's to the sons of Saint David,
Those youngsters so loyal and keen
Who'll haul down the red, white and blue, lads,
And hoist up the red, white and green.

In the dark gloomy days of December
We mourn for Llywelyn with pride
Who fell in defence of his country
With eighteen brave men by his side.

So here's to the sons of Llywelyn,
The heirs of that valiant eighteen
Who'll haul down the red, white and blue, lads,
And hoist up the red, white and green.

In the warm, golden days of September,
Great Owain Glyndŵr took the field,
For fifteen long years did he struggle
And never the dragon did yield.

So here's to the sons of Great Owain,
Who'll show the proud Sais what we mean
When we haul down the red, white and blue, lads,
And hoist up the red, white and green.

There are many more names to remember
And some that will never be known
Who were loyal to Wales and the gwerin
And defied all the might of the throne.

So here's to the sons of the gwerin
Who care not for prince or for queen,
Who'll haul down the red, white and blue, lads,
And hoist up the red, white and green!

Cywydd o Fawl

yn null y gogogynfeirdd à gogo

Flap we our lips, praise Big Man,
Bards religious shire Cardigan.
Not frogs croaking are we
Nor vain crows but bards tidy.
Wise is our speak, like Shadrach,
Hearken you now, people bach.
Mouth some, Cardiff ach y fi,
Not holy like Aberteifi.
Twp it is to speech so,
In Cardiff is gold yellow,
Truth it is and no fable,
All for bards respectable.
White Jesus bach, let no ill
Befall Big Heads Arts Council.
Pounds they have, many thousand,
Like full till shop draper grand.
Good is the work they are at,
Soaped they shall be in Seiat,
Reserved shall be for them
A place in Big Seat Salem.
Praised let them be for this thing,
Money they are distributing
Like Beibl Moses his manna.
Tongue we all, bards Welsh, Ta!

Merlin's Prophecy

One day, when Wales is free and prosperous
And dull, they'll all be wishing they were us.

Snap

Mr Richardson the plumber was old. His brass plate
Had been polished every morning for so many years
That all the lettering had been rubbed off. But his face
Between bowler and collar was ploughed deep. We
                                            thought
He was the oldest man in the world, would linger
                                            from school
In his workshop of thrilling smells and shapes,
                                            solder,
Tallow, flux, spigot-joints, stillsons, shavehooks,
                                            ladles,
Splashsticks, reamers and ball valves. He had
                            learnt his trade
Building the hospital, the cuckoo-clock schloss
Of sprouting spires that swam in an enchanted
                                            atmosphere
Of disinfectant and chloroform at the end of the
                                            street.
He remembered too the laying of the railway line
Along the bay, the whitewashed fisher cottages in
                                            the dunes

Where now the coaltrucks clanked their iron rosary.
His faded eyes had seen, his old brain held a
                                    memory of
The seashore Landor roamed, the lonely windy
Reaches of sand and wild roses, where the kites
                                    screamed,
And where we knew the cricket field and tram
                                    terminus,
Cows grazing in meadows that had not changed
Since the long ships made landfall.

One night during the war, a Yank screwed a girl
So savagely in Mr Richardson's front garden
That she died on his doorstep.

Gwenallt

When I heard he was dead
I remembered so many things:
A little man speaking in the rain
To a soaked crowd with bedraggled flags
Around the mediocre monumental masonry
That is Pantycelyn's grave.
I remembered the bite, the corgi snarl
Of the pencerdd blasting his enemies.
I remembered reading for the first time
In a language I hardly knew
Words that have guided my feet
To the sacred places, the voice that led me
To inmost Wales.
                                        It was Christmas Eve,
The feast of trash and tinsel, the streets
All slush and spew, the cash registers
Ringing Glory to Mammon in the Highest.
I remembered, it was somehow relevant,
The old men of Dowlais reminiscing
About the colliers coming out of the cwbs
At Cae Harris Station, men, they said,
With ninety per cent dust who could hit Top C
As if it never existed –
And all the memories slammed me in the guts.

The Next Village to Manafon

It was half-past seven on Saturday night
When we stopped off at The Powys Arms.
Already the locals were half-way tight,
Red-faced men from the steep green farms.

Some talked of girls and country pleasures
And some were grumbling about the hay
And some were discussing the bardic measures,
Heirs of Owain Cyfeiliog they.

We kept our end up, passing strangers,
As best we could, with what tales we knew,
Avoiding the subtle verbal dangers
Laid like poachers by the deft-tongued crew.

Song for song we joined in the singing
And not for a moment the clonc did flag,
The glasses clinked and the room was ringing.
I hope God drinks, said the village wag.

It was half-past nine on Saturday night
As we broke the spell and drove over the hill.
They pressed us to stay, but we took our flight
And none too soon, or we'd be there still.

A Crown for Branwen

I pluck now an image out of a far
Past and a far place, counties away
On the wrong side of Severn, acres
Of alien flint and chalk, the smooth hills
Subtly, unmistakeably English, different.
I remember, as if they were China, Sinodun,
Heaven's Gate and Angel Down, the White Horse
Hidden from the eye of war, Alfred at Wantage,
His bodyguard of four Victorian lamp-posts
And his country waiting for another enemy
Who did not come that summer. Everything
Shone in the sun, the burnished mail of wheat
And hot white rock, but mostly I recall
The long trench.

      A thousand years from now
They'll find the line of it, they'll tentatively
Make scholarly conjectures relating it
To Wansdyke, the Icknield Way, Silbury.
They'll never have known a summer
Of tense expectancy that drove
A desperate gash across England
To stop the tanks.

      Most clearly I see
The tumbled ramparts of frantic earth
Hastily thrown up, left to the drifting

Seeds of the waste, and the poppies,
Those poppies, that long slash of red
Across the shining corn, a wound, a wonder.

Lady, your land's invaded, we have thrown
Hurried defences up, our soil is raw,
New, shallow, the old crops do not grow
Here where we man the trench. I bring
No golden-armoured wheat, the delicate dance
Of oats to the harvest is not for me nor
The magic spears of barley, on this rough stretch
Only the poppies thrive. I wreathe for you
A crown of wasteland flowers, let them blaze
A moment in the midnight of your hair
And be forgotten when the coulter drives
A fertile furrow over our old wars
For the strong corn, our children's bread.
Only, Princess, I ask that when you bring
Those bright sheaves to the altar, and you see
Some random poppies tangled there, you'll smile,
As women do, remembering dead love.

The Meeting

You couldn't have got much further up the valley,
The hills behind us were a steep green wall
And all the folk were talkative and pally
As they crowded to the meeting at the hall.

We're very glad to see you here, they told us,
We don't get many coming from outside,
As they steered us past the pot-holes, sheep and
                                                boulders,
The most interesting thing since Mabon died.

The schoolroom where we spoke was neat but
                                                dowdy,
The chairman knew the people all by name,
The heckling, on the whole, was not too rowdy,
They knew the rules and they enjoyed the game.

And then, under the stars, it somehow started
As the audience drifted to the street outside
As to and fro the dialectic darted,
For some were for and some against the Blaid.

Long-tethered tempers rose like boiling custard,
The quarrel echoed from the high dark hill,
Young men were passionate and old men blustered,
The girls, alas, were vehement and shrill.

And some who saw us off were rather nettled –
We don't know why you've come here, for a start.
Before tonight we were all so nicely settled,
Now you've gone and blown the bloody place apart.

Never Again

You never saw such a stupid mess,
The government, of course, was to blame.
That poor young kid in her shabby dress
And the old chap with her, it seemed such a shame.

She had the baby in a backyard shed,
It wasn't very nice, but the best we could do.
Just fancy, a manger for a bed,
I ask you, what's the world coming to?

We're sorry they had to have it so rough,
But we had our troubles, too, remember,
As if all the crowds were not enough
The weather was upside-down for December.

There was singing everywhere, lights in the sky
And those drunken shepherds neglecting their sheep
And three weird foreigners in full cry –
You just couldn't get a good night's sleep.

Well now they've gone we can all settle down,
There's room at the inn and the streets are so still
And we're back to normal in our own little town
That nobody's heard of, or ever will.

And though the world's full of people like those,
I think of them sometimes, especially her,
And one can't help wondering . . . though I don't
                                    suppose
Anyone will ever know who they were.

Bi-Centenary

Cut daffodils, the topography
Of the Lake District, Batsford's
English Countryside in Ektachrome,
Anthologies, tight little bunches
Of cut lyrics wilting. Lives
By eminent scholars. This is
The two-hundredth anniversary
Of William Wordsworth, poet,
Ancient Monument, valuable asset
To the tourist industry, indispensable
Ingredient in Education, conditioning
Town kids to think that poetry
Is all about clouds, cuckoos
And bloody daffodils. Stale
From over-exposure, the words
Will not come alive. I do my best,
It's no good, they've got him.
Here lies William Wordsworth
Killed by colour-supplements,
Murdered by thesis, buried
Under a cairn of footnotes
Piled high and heavy to keep under
The shouting madman, the seer,
The stranger, priest of darkness.

Three Parodies

1
Dai Dripp: Elegy for a Fried Egg

You should have heard me the other night
Railing at shoddy materialism and the price of grub
In a phony pretentious restaurant in Queen Street
Where the soup came out of a tin and the pâté
maison
Was bought at the supermarket, one of those places
Frequented by secondhand car salesmen,
That fine flower of the Welsh metropolis
And their expensive kept bitches.
Christ, how I told them a thing or two, while my
grandfather
Keeled over on to the cheeseboard from sheer
decrepitude.
As they chucked me out I thought of Rilke,
That homosexual French dwarf who cut his ear off
And ran away to Tahiti,
I thought of Captain Cook who set sail
From the lake in Roath Park and discovered
Patagonia.
I though of Miss Pugh next door but one
And her big tits. Then I went home
And wrote a poem about a hamster
Before catching a diesel to death.

2

Susan Spam: Recipe for Success

Hubby was cleaning the mini
And I was making a flan,
Cuddles was eating her Weetybits
When suddenly I had a plan
To supplement the housekeeping
And keep up with the folks in the road
By having a bash at poetry
And running up an ode
As neat as a good-class semi,
Brisk, cheerful and bright
But with just that touch of meaning
That makes it sound all right.
Nothing deep or gloomy,
No boring political guff,
But cleaning and shopping and babies,
Sensible wholesome stuff.
And I sent it to an editor
Whose name, I'm afraid, I forget
But he lives in the right part of Cardiff
And I'm told he's rather a pet.
And I'm terribly glad I tried it,
And Hubby is pleased as well.
For it's much more fun than knitting
And awfully easy to sell.
So, all suburban housewives
You won't find the job too hard,

Take five minutes off from the housework
And you too can be a bard.

3
Ianto Rhydderch: Tch Tch

One day while I was docking swedes
With a slow moronic grin
And all my ancestors' misdeeds
Wrought their sour death within,

Suddenly there came into view
A figure gaunt and tall.
He said, Forgive me naming you.
I made no sound at all.

He carried on at tedious length
About my life so grim,
It took all my idiot peasant strength
To be polite to him.

At last he ceased and strode away,
The cold Welsh rain came down,
In puddles in that barren clay
I watched my country drown.

Then, indistinguishable from mud,
I started my old car,

The sickness of my tainted blood
Inclined me to a jar.

And oh what festering itch of sin
Brought this damp thought to me
As I fuddled in a squalid inn:
Un bain't much help to we.

Waldo

I had my photo taken with him once
In a pub in Pontarddulais but
Paul Riley didn't twist the spool before
Taking the next snap, the only picture
He ever spoilt. So now I have no record
Of that summer meeting.

       Yes, Waldo,
It was always summer when I met you –
You are my personal Bardd yr Haf –
An eisteddfod or a conference, a froth
Of holiday and high endeavour your presence
Turned to wine. Not your rare words
You had already spoken. We gathered
Under the leaves of the tree, the light
Interpreted.

       Llangollen Bridge, not even
The tourist industry can cheapen it, but
For me it's where we first met, talked
About nothing much, made contact. I had
Nothing in common really with this
Quaker, pacifist, mystic, cywyddwr,
A better poet and a better man,
Someone I might have been like with luck
And effort, but am not. That botched snapshot
Ten years ago is the true symbol;
Not even the best painter I've known
Could put us in the same picture.

The Rock and the Book

Flood-lit, the rock of the Gododdin floats
Above the shops and bars. Valhalla? No,
More like the island of Laputa, incompatible
With the real world, lovely for a festival
But only scenery after all. Stick it up there,
Forget about it, they say, another people
Turning its back on their history, wallowing
In the mere present. The old city is not quite
A morgue or a museum, Deacon Brodie, Montrose,
John Knox, Mary Stuart and David Hume
Are still here, just. Feel the psychic wind
Of their passing in the Lawnmarket, or is it only
The cold air sneaking in from the sea?
Is there anyone here at all? Emptiness echoes
Even when there are people about. This
Is what it is like to be a former capital.
The old parliament building is closed for repairs.
Why bother? The Turks were kinder to Athens
And the Russians to Prague. There at least
There was no pretence.

Wade through the jettisoned centuries, prod
For silted relics, read in a glass case
Letters by dead hands, archive of a dead kingdom.
Our language was spoken here once, and here
Our literature began, chanted on those ramparts
Whose magic is dependent on a switch
That can be turned off at any time.

Return
To a country whose chief city has no intrusive
Dramatic thrust of rock at its flat centre, built
Mostly on sand and mud. There in an iron box,
In an ugly building, they hide an old brown book
The colour of seaweed. You wouldn't look at it twice
Unless you knew, unless you knew.

That Summer

The first thing I remember is the General Strike,
My father in his shirt-sleeves leaning on the front
gate
Smoking his pipe in the sunshine,
Miss Davies the shop calling across to him,
Are you out, Mr Webb? I hear now
Her bright amused voice, see Catherine Street
Empty and clean, hear the nine days' silence
As the last ripple of a lost revolution
Ebbed into history and the long defeat
Began to mass its shadows. The ambulances
Were absent from the road beside the hospital,
Garn Goch Number Three, Great Mountain,
Gilbertsons,
Elba, the names I learnt to read by, names
Of collieries and tinworks, names of battlefields
Where a class and a nation surrendered
The summer they killed Wales.

We spent the time on the sands, played all day.
We had the whole place to ourselves,
Or so it has always seemed, from the West Pier
To Vivian Stream. When you are five years old
There are things you understand more easily
Than ever afterwards, that the sea is huge
And goes on for ever from Swansea, the moon
And the hospital clock inhabit the same sky,

Neighbours. But there are other things, and these
You only understand later, much later.
Inland, in those ambulance villages, the other side
Of Town Hill, from stations further up the line
From Mumbles Road, already it was beginning,
The losers' trek, the haemorrhage of our future.
But for a child there is only the present.
Dad, I said, there'd be lovely if the strike
Was all the time, then you and me could come
Down the sands every day and play. He laughed.
It wouldn't do, son, he said, it wouldn't do,
There's got to be work, see, there's got to be work.
Chasing a ball, I didn't stop to argue, forgot
I'd ever asked the question till later, long after
The summer my country died.

Abbey Cwmhir

Cow-pasture and the ragged line
Of a ruined wall. A few more cartloads
Of dressed stone filched for a new farmhouse
Or sections of clustered column taken for a
                              cheese-press
And there would be nothing, less even
Than these scrappy remains under the big trees.
The coffin-lid of an old abbot is propped up
Behind the door of the Victorian church,
That's all. Heavy with July, the elms
Remember nothing.

                    Appropriately
There is no signpost, not even a field-path
To the place where they brought the hacked trunk.
Who were they, I wonder, who lugged him here,
All that was left of him, after the English
Had done their thing, what went on in their minds,
Conventional piety, simple human pity
Or the cosmic grief the Son of the Red Judge
Sang in the stormwind, as they urged the pony
Felted with its winter coat, and over the crupper
The bloody carcase, along the bad ways?

Centuries later, in high summer, I feel the cold.

Advice to a Young Poet

Sing for Wales or shut your trap –
All the rest's a load of crap.

To a Reader

Yes, you have heard, and turned away
Unheeding from the songs I've sung,
For you my tunes have had their day
And I am dead and you are young.

Yours is the country I would see
Beyond the age's endless night,
Half-heedless of its liberty
That's yours by custom and by right.

And there, maybe, on some dark shelf
Or in a tedious book at school
Lingers a little of myself
For you to smile at as a fool

Who wasted all his scanty powers
Harping on grudges, hopes and wrongs,
And you will say, He's none of ours,
Today we sing far different songs.

Let it be so, and I am glad.
I only sang of what I knew,
Your world is bright where ours is sad
And what are all our griefs to you?

And so you throw my book aside,
A tale of best forgotten days,
You who are free and walk in pride –
For me, it is a form of praise.

The Emigrants

They started walking from Llanbrynmair,
Men going ahead, women and children following,
To Carmarthen quay, but were warned in time,
The press gang are in town. The men turned east
And walked to Bristol. The women and children
Boarded ship, were wrecked on Llansteffan sands.
Stumbling ashore, they too turned east, walked to
                                        Bristol.
Some died. When at last they set sail
They were six stormy weeks at sea.
Landing, they resumed their walk: the length of
                                        Pennsylvania
Over the Alleghenies through the Cumberland Gap
To the headwaters of the Ohio. Down the Great
                                        Valley then
On rafts, made fast to the bank each night, until
They came to Paddy's Run. Frenchmen (where was
                                        Paddy?)
Welcomed them, pressed them to stay. No,
They must walk yet further, Kentucky was waiting.
Evansville, Hopkinsville, Owensboro,
Tall corn, deep grass, land that grew everything
Except landlords. Next morning, though, their rafts
                                        were gone,
The moorings cut in the night. They stayed. They
                                        had to.

On those luminous plains there are thirty gathered
                                                    churches
Where the gods of Wales are worshipped. Once a
                                                       year
They have a Gymanfa Ganu and good luck to them.
One only asks, hearing the tale told,
Why did they have to walk so far?
In the name of all their gods and ours,
What were they walking away from?

Day Out

Up the Golden Valley
Sunday afternoon
Kenderchurch and Michaelchurch
Michaelmas is soon

Up the Golden Valley
Season nearly done
Every ripening apple
Is a golden sun

Up through Ewyas Harold
Stop at Abbey Dore
Admire the church restored by
Viscount Scudamore

Where the road climbs steeply
Pause and view the scene
Woods and fields and orchards
Down to Bredwardine

Dorstone, Bacton, Vowchurch
At the end of day
Peterchurch and Cusop
Cup of tea at Hay

Cabalva, Cliffordd, Clyro
Where the Wye-mist swirls
The ghost of Parson Kilvert
Is chasing little girls

Huge against the sunset
Hills of home stand stark
Gently now on Ewyas
Dewfall, dusk and dark

Sell-out

There was this film, see, the ultimate epic,
Starring at vast expense, Sir Richard ap Surd
Fresh from his triumph in *The Four Horsemen of the
Acropolis*
And the versatile Irish beauty Nymph O'Maniac,
Supported by an impressive cast recruited
From all the out-of-work actors in Cardiff
And a chorus of singing sheep.
Script by the same talented team that gave us
My Soul is a Slagheap and *Bash Him with your Harp,
Butty,*

Portraying with brutal realistic candour,
Suffused, of course, with gentle, wistful lyricism,
The pride, the passion, the heartbreak,
The goings-on and the gettings-up-to
Of our picturesque people, with extra dialogue
Specially lent by the Welsh Joke Museum.
It was called *The Rains of Rhondda*, so naturally
It was shot at Ebbw Vale. On the first day
The camera crew were drowned when the sewers
burst,

Most of the cast were incapacitated for life
After a punch-up at the Puddlers' Arms
And the leading lady couldn't be prised apart
From the front row of the First XV.
They retreated in confusion, fantasy
As always in Wales swamped by the reality.

It was finished at last in Egypt
With the Pyramids disguised as coaltips
And the Sphinx made up to look like Lloyd George
And shown at the Lucrezia Borgia Memorial Film
                                        Festival.
Drooled the Arts Page of our National Newspaper:
It was as if Eisenstein had transcribed the Football
                                        Echo,
A triumph, a total experience, my bowels were
                                        moved.
The losses are estimated at an equivalent sum
To the entire gross national product of Outer
                                        Mongolia.

The Stars of Mexico

They call me Jack the Fifer and I come from
                            Nantyglo,
And I played my fife for freedom not so many
                            years ago,
When we took the People's Charter to the gates of
                          Newport town,
When we marched to win a Kingdom, and the
                          soldiers shot us down.
And sometimes I remember the grey skies of
                          Nantyglo
As I spread my trooper's blanket 'neath the stars of
                          Mexico.

In green and gracious valleys among the hills of
                          Gwent
We never saw the sunshine, to earth our backs were
                          bent,
Like a toiling slave an early grave was all we had to
                          gain,
So we struck like men and struck again, but our
                          struggle was in vain.
And sometimes I remember how we dealt that final
                          blow
As I march to other battles 'neath the stars of Mexico.

The month it was November and all the storm
                              winds blew,
And as we marched to Newport, full many of us
                              knew
That our comrades would be lying at the rising of
                              the sun
Who'd never feel its warmth again, nor hear our
                              rivers run.
But we shouldered pike and musket as onward we
                              did go
And we marched as bold as any in the wars of
                              Mexico.

They'd have hanged me as a traitor, so I crossed the
                              stormy sea
And I play my fife in a better life in the Land of
                              Liberty.
For the cruel laws of England I do not give a damn
And I'm shouldering my rifle 'neath the flag of
                              Uncle Sam,
And I'm marching as a soldier in the War of Mexico
To a place I've never heard of, and it's called the
                              Alamo.

They call me Jack the Fifer and I come from
                              Nantyglo.
I always was a fighter and I'll always strike a blow.
With the Stars and Stripes above me, I'll make a
                              soldier's stand

And not disgrace my ancient race, nor dear Wales,
                                   my native land,
And I'll take her honour with me, though fate may
                                        lay me low
Far distant from my homeland, 'neath the stars of
                                          Mexico.

Our Scientists are Working on it

What Wales needs, and has always lacked most
Is, instead of an eastern boundary, an East Coast.

For further reading

Poems:
The Green Desert (Gomer, 1969)
A Crown for Branwen (Gomer, 1974)
Rampage and Revel (Gomer, 1977)
Poems and Pints (Gomer, 1983)
Collected Poems (Gomer, 1995)
Looking up England's Arsehole (Y Lolfa, 2000)

Prose:
No Half-Way House: selected political journalism
  (Y Lolfa, 1998)
A Militant Muse (Seren, 1998)

Criticism:
Brian Morris, *Harri Webb* in the *Writers of Wales*
  series (1993)

Images of Wales

The Corgi Series covers, no.17
'Gwinllan' by Gareth Owen

Gareth Owen
1965-1970 Cardiff College of Art
1970-1973 Art Teacher Ysgol Gyfun Rhydfelen
1973-1983 Art Teacher Ysgol y Berwyn, Y Bala
1983-   Head of Art Ysgol y Creuddyn
1997-   Shares the above post with Art Teacher
            Adviser for Cynnal
Designing for the stage:
Set designs for Cwmni Theatr Maldwyn:
Y Mab Darogan (Adapted for television)
Y Llew a'r Ddraig
Y Cylch
Pum Diwrnod o Ryddid (Adapted for television)
Heledd (Adapted for television)
Cwmni Ieuenctid Meirion:
Er Mwyn Yfory (Pavilion stage Eisteddfod
Genedlaethol Meirion and a tour of Wales)
Eisteddfod Drama Company – Eisteddfod
Genedlaethol Porthmadog:
Gwas a Dau Feistr – Theatr Ardudwy Harlech
Cwmni Ieuenctid yr Urdd Bro Conwy:
Ail Liwio'r Byd (North Wales Theatre)
Recent one-man shows:
Oriel Theatr Ardudwy
Oriel Plas Glyn y Weddw, Llanbedrog
Oriel Llyfrgell Caernarfon